THE

DISTRACT YOURSELF

DISTRACT YOURSELF

101 positive things to do and learn before the end of the world

sphere

SPHERE

First published in Great Britain in 2020 by Sphere

1 3 5 7 9 10 8 6 4 2

A CIP catalogue record for this book
is available from the British Library.

ISBN paperback: 978-0-7515-8148-5
ISBN ebook: 978-0-7515-8147-8

Typeset by M Rules
Printed and bound in Great Britain by
Clays Ltd, Elcograf S.p.A.

Papers used by Sphere are from well-managed forests
and other responsible sources.

MIX
Paper from
responsible sources
FSC® C104740

Sphere
An imprint of
Little, Brown Book Group
Carmelite House,
50 Victoria Embankment
London EC4Y 0DZ

An Hachette UK Company
www.hachette.co.uk

www.littlebrown.co.uk

For you; whoever you are, wherever you're from

HOLA! (AND HOW TO USE THIS BOOK)

Whether our worries are personal, political or global-shaped, we all need to drop them at the door from time to time and give our brains a holiday. And that is exactly what this book is here for: 101 simple, fun, smart, silly, useful, good-to-know, short bursts of positive activities and facts to engage with when you need a break from the troubles life is throwing at you. And if you're feeling easy breezy but just a tad bored? They're still perfect for you too! Whether it's a quiz, an anagram, an idea to pursue outside of this book or a poem about cats, we've got you covered with boredom-busting ideas.

Consume this book however you like; you can start in the middle or at the end if you so choose, or you might like to flick back and forth. It may be that you'd like to use it for some quiet 'me' time, or you may prefer to get your friends and family involved – whatever works for you works for us and all the activities within are family-friendly.

All you need to enjoy it is a bit of time and some nice deep breaths, but some pen and paper/the notes section on your phone will come in useful for a few of the activities. You might also find yourself inspired to go down some internet rabbit holes in search of more information; we love curiosity in the

Distract Yourself camp and would actively encourage you to do this.

However you choose to absorb it, we hope this book provides the tonic you need to feel calm, inspired and a bit more positive about whatever's going on around you.

1
AGE ON THE STAGE

What/who is older?

A) Machu Picchu in Peru or the Taj Mahal in India?
B) The Eiffel Tower in Paris or the Empire State Building in New York?
C) Donald Trump or Vladimir Putin?
D) Justin Bieber or Harry Styles?
E) Sydney Opera House in Australia or the Lotus Temple in Delhi?
F) Angkor Wat in Cambodia or St Basil's Cathedral in Russia?
G) Buckingham Palace in London or Palace of Versailles outside Paris?
H) Leaning Tower of Pisa in Italy or the Forbidden City in China?
I) J. K. Rowling or Neil Gaiman?
J) Beyoncé or David Beckham?

2
UNSCRAMBLE THIS ANAGRAM!

MACHO PIN
(What you'll be once
you've got this)

3

PARROT POWER

Learn, write out or send on this quote:

'I wish it need not have happened in my time,' said Frodo.

'So do I,' said Gandalf, 'And so do all who live to see such times. But that is not for them to decide. All we have to decide is what to do with the time that is given us.'

J. R. R. Tolkien wrote this in his masterpiece, *The Fellowship of the Ring*, which was first published in 1954

QUIZ CORNER: SPACE

A) Which is the hottest planet in our solar system?
B) Which galaxy is the Milky Way due to collide with in 3.75 billion years?
C) Why is Pluto no longer considered a planet?
D) How old do we think the Sun is?
E) When do we think the Big Bang happened and how do we know?
F) What was the first artificial satellite successfully launched into space, and what did it trigger?
G) If you managed to fly to Jupiter, why wouldn't you be able to land on it?
H) Why will the footprints left by the astronauts who walked on the moon back in 1969 still be there?
I) What planet in our solar system has mesmerising rings of water and ice (along with a few rocks) orbiting around it?
J) What does 'Hubble' refer to?

5

FACT ATTACK!

Learn this gem and wow people
with your genius

The supercontinent that existed 175 million years ago, before the continents split apart, is known as Pangea, and the super ocean that surrounded it is known as Panthalassa. Pangea is constructed from the Ancient Greek for 'all' (Pan) and 'Mother Earth' (Gaia). Similarly, Panthalassa means 'all sea'.

RIDDLE ME THIS:

What has two hands
and a face but no eyes,
nose or mouth?

7

POETRY CORNER

Learn, write out or send on the below:

I Wandered Lonely as a Cloud
William Wordsworth

I wandered lonely as a cloud
That floats on high o'er vales and hills,
When all at once I saw a crowd,
A host, of golden daffodils;
Beside the lake, beneath the trees,
Fluttering and dancing in the breeze.

Continuous as the stars that shine
And twinkle on the milky way,
They stretched in never-ending line
Along the margin of a bay:
Ten thousand saw I at a glance,
Tossing their heads in sprightly dance.

The waves beside them danced; but they
Out-did the sparkling waves in glee:
A poet could not but be gay,
In such a jocund company:

I gazed – and gazed – but little thought
What wealth the show to me had brought:

For oft, when on my couch I lie
In vacant or in pensive mood,
They flash upon that inward eye
Which is the bliss of solitude;
And then my heart with pleasure fills,
And dances with the daffodils.

Fun fact: Wordsworth was inspired to write this poem in April 1802, after he saw a long belt of daffodils with his sister Dorothy on a walk in the Lake District in England.

8
WORD SPLURGE

Make as many different words as you can from the following letters:

YOU CAN DO ANYTHING

AROUND THE WORLD

Learn how to say 'Nice to meet you' in other languages

Portuguese: Prazer em conhecê-lo
🔊 pra-zeer em con-gnee-say-low

Russian: Приятно встретить тебя (Priyatno vstretit' tebya)
🔊 Pree-yat-nos-tree-tit teb-yer

Japanese: はじめまして (Hajimemashite)
🔊 Ha-jee-mem-mass-tyet

Romanian: Încântat de cunoștință
🔊 in-kern-tat de coo-nosh-tinta

Dutch: Aangenaam kennis te maken
🔊 An-ger-nam ken-niss ter marken

Italian: piacere di conoscerti
🔊 Pee-atch-ee-airy di con-ohsh-share-tee

TELL SOMEONE THIS JOKE:

Why was the donkey sent to
bed without dinner?

He wouldn't stop horsing around!

FIRST AMONG FOLKS

The first circumnavigation of the world took place 500 years ago by Portuguese explorers, who set out in September 1519 in the hope of finding a quicker way of getting to the East Indies (modern-day Indonesia) by sailing west rather than east. The captain was Ferdinand Magellan; he managed to sail his crew across the mighty Atlantic Ocean, down the east coast of South America, through a strait at the bottom of the continent and over the mighty expanse of the Pacific Ocean – but he was killed by natives on the Philippine island of Mactan so didn't make it home. However, three years after setting sail, one ship from the expedition did arrive safely back, although only eighteen of the 260 original crew had survived!

12

POP THIS BOOK DOWN AND . . .

. . . Practise your skills of observation – you can do this either with a person who's near you or on the TV. Imagine you want to describe that person to a friend who will never meet or see this person you're looking at. How would you build a picture of the person for your friend? What face shape do they have? Do the colour of their eyes remind you of anything? What else can you think of that matches the colour of their skin? What are the patterns on their clothes? What's the tone of their voice? Do they fidget when they speak, or use hand gestures? What conclusions are you drawing about their personality?

13

WHAT DID YOU SAY?

**Translate the below word using the
Morse Code dictionary:**

●▬ ▬● ●▬●● ●▬ ▬●▬● ▬ ●●▬● ●● ▬ ●▬ ●●

QUIZ CORNER: MATHS

A) Which of these is *not* a prime number? 5, 47, 61, 91, 163

B) What's the square root of 1089?

C) Suzanne has £10 to buy some sweets for her and her family. A bar of chocolate is £1, a pack of gummy bears is 80p and a pack of strawberry laces is 50p. Suzanne buys two bars of chocolate and five packs of gummy bears. With the leftover change, how many packs of strawberry laces can she buy?

D) Imran has gone on a nice flat bike ride. For the first half an hour he travelled at 10mph, then for the next fifteen minutes he travelled at 12mph, and then for the last half an hour he travelled at 5mph. What distance has he travelled?

E) Which is the smaller fraction: 7/9 or 6/8?

F) A pile of books on a coffee table measures 15cm in height. The measurement between the top of the book pile to the top of a book that is on the floor is 55cm. The book on the floor is moved to the top of the pile of books on the coffee table. The measurement from the top of the books to the floor is now 75cm. How tall is the book that was on the floor? And how tall is the table?

G) What degrees are all the internal angles on an equilateral triangle?

H) What is $(99 \times 15)^2 - ((1589 \times 1385) - 4460)$?

WHEN INVENTIVE INVENTIONS WERE INVENTED

BCE:

3500: The wheel
3000: Papyrus, a
      predecessor of paper
2000: Machinery that could
      lift heavy objects using
      counterweights
400: Water wheel
300-200: Compasses
      (although not used for
      navigation for another
      thousand years)
250: The lighthouse
150: Paper

CE:

62: Steam power
800: Windmills
800: Gunpowder and
     fireworks

1450: Modern printing press
1596: Flushing toilet
1698: Binary number system
      (still used today in the
      majority of computers)
1700s: Piano
1714: Thermometer
1783: First practical hot air
      balloon
1800s: Pasteurisation
1814: First practical steam
      locomotive
1830s-1840s: Electric telegraph
1876: Telephone
1880: Life Raft
1886: Dishwasher
1888: First commercial camera
1901: Vacuum cleaner
1908: The first affordable car
1920s: Television
1927: First popular home
      refrigerator
1930s: Ballpoint pen

1951: Barcode

1965: Portable defibrillator

1968: World's first solar power station

1973: First mobile phone

1982: The CD

1989: World wide web

2001: iPod

2001: Wikipedia

2007: Kindle

LEARN

16
UNSCRAMBLE THIS ANAGRAM!

EFFECTS NERVE

(A bubbly word for a

vivacious individual)

17
MEMORISE THE MOON

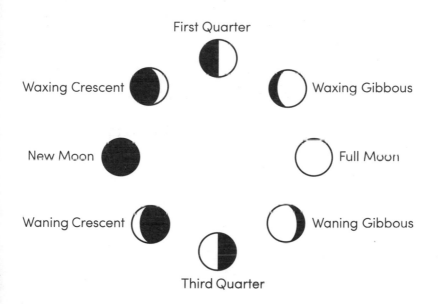

First Quarter

Waxing Crescent

Waxing Gibbous

New Moon

Full Moon

Waning Crescent

Waning Gibbous

Third Quarter

18
RIDDLE ME THIS:

What has branches
but no leaves?

IF THE HISTORY OF THE EARTH HAPPENED IN ONE DAY ...

00:10: Earth collides with the planet Theia, flinging off a bit of rock that turns into the moon.

04:00: Life starts! For now just single-celled organisms.

05:30: The single-celled organisms are going berserk in the oceans, feasting on the methane in the atmosphere and multiplying as a result.

11:00: Oxygen fills the atmosphere from all the photosynthesising bacteria.

11:35: The whole world freezes over.

13:00: Everything melts and life is getting more complicated: internal organs are forming inside certain cells.

16:00: The cells with internal organs very slowly start to divide into funghi, plants and animals.

19:20: Sponges in the ocean arrive!

19:45: Placozoa – the last common ancestor of all animals on Earth – develop.

19:55: The world freezes over for a second time.

20:20: Freeze done with, seaweed and jellyfish are chilling in the ocean.

21:00: Vertebrates have arrived!

21:11: Some of the animals in the sea crawl out onto the land, and plants on land start growing.

21:41: Insects take off!

21:45: The first four-legged animals evolve in shallow waters.

22:30: A mystery causes a major extinction and only 5 per cent of species survive.

22:34: Here come the dinosaurs!

22:45: Another minute, another mystery and another mass extinction takes place – but dinosaurs survive.

23:00: Birds are here!

23:26: The asteroid that wipes out the dinosaurs hits, meaning mammals can start taking over.

23:30: Primates are evolving.

23:59: With only tens of seconds left to go, humans arrive!

20

QUIZ CORNER: HISTORY

D
O

A) Which empire did Genghis Khan begin back in 1206?
B) When did the first settlers in New Zealand arrive from Polynesia?
C) How old are the pyramids?
D) What were the two sides in the American Civil War called?
E) What is Bastille Day?
F) Which city was England's original capital?
G) Who was Cheng I Sao?
H) Which country saw the Inca Empire flourish in the 13th to the 16th centuries?
I) When did Apartheid in South Africa end?
J) When did the Berlin Wall come down?

FACT ATTACK

Learn this gem and wow people with your genius

Hardly any flags of the countries of the world feature purple. This isn't because purple was unfashionable, but because until more recent times, purple dyes were incredibly expensive. Until the 19th century, there were very few ways to make the dye needed and the main way involved using a species of sea snail that lived in the Mediterranean. You needed 10,000 snails to make a single gram of purple dye! Hence it being too costly to pop on a flag. Thankfully now we have synthetic purple dyes and don't have to rely on any poor snails.

AROUND THE WORLD

Can you name these countries?

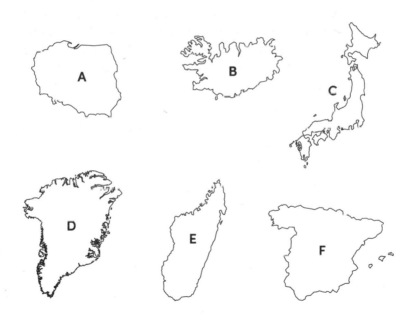

WORD SPLURGE!

Make as many different words as you can from the following letters:

THIS TOO SHALL PASS

EXPAND YOUR LEXICON:

Apricate (verb): to bask in the sun

Finifugal (adjective): a person who is finifugal avoids or prolongs endings and final moments e.g. goodbyes or the last few pages of a book

Lalochezia (noun): experiencing pleasure or relieving pain by swearing

Quiddle (verb): To waffle, or waste time by doing unimportant, non-urgent things

Bibliosmia (noun): The enjoyment of smelling a book

Respair (noun/verb): the period of time after despair, when hope returns

25

POP THIS BOOK DOWN AND . . .

. . . Write down the lyrics of your favourite upbeat song – this can be on a scrap of paper, or alternatively you could write out your favourite line or verse in a calligraphy-style way. Prop the paper up against your mirror or stick it on the fridge so you can see it each day.

UNSCRAMBLE THIS ANAGRAM!

HI AMOURS NO

(We're all in this together)

27

MARRY, KISS OR SELFIE

Prince Harry, Justin Trudeau and Prince Nikolai of Denmark

Olivia Colman, Gwyneth Paltrow and Chrissy Teigen

Idris Elba, Mila Kunis and Leonardo DiCaprio

Sandra Oh, Jodie Comer and Phoebe Waller-Bridge

Zac Efron, Hugh Jackman and Dev Patel

Halle Berry, Paul Dano and Scarlett Johansson

Chiwetel Ejiofor, Robert Downey Jr. and Vincent Rodriguez

Shakira, Jennifer Lopez and Madonna

Daniel Craig, Pierce Brosnan and Roger Moore

Taylor Swift, Rihanna and Penelope Cruz

George W Bush, Barack Obama and Donald Trump

28

PARROT POWER

Learn, write out or send on this quote:

'Doubt is the origin of wisdom'

The French philosopher, mathematician and scientist René Descartes wrote this (in Latin) in the 17th Century.

QUIZ CORNER: BOOKS

A) Who was the first woman to be awarded the Booker Prize twice?
B) What is the name of George Orwell's protagonist in *1984*?
C) Which book series talks of Dust, daemons and armoured bears?
D) Which book became the first eBook, published in 1971?
E) 'I write this sitting in the kitchen sink' is the famous first line of which book by Dodie Smith?
F) The longest sentence ever printed is 823 words. Which book is it in?
G) Who invented the characters Miss Trunchbull, Violet Beauregarde and Mr Twit?
H) When was the first Harry Potter published?
I) Who was Hans Christian Andersen?
J) What is the bestselling book of all time?

30

AROUND THE WORLD

How to say 'How are you?' in other languages

Afrikaans:
Hoe gaan dit?
🦻 Who garn dit

Arabic:
كيف حالك (**kayf halik?**)
🦻 Kay-fer ha-lee-kee

Albanian:
Si jeni?
🦻 See ee-any

Hindu:
क्या हाल है (**kya haal hai?**)
🦻 Kee-ya haal hay

Swedish:
Hur mår du?
🦻 Hir more der

German:
Wie Gehts?
🦻 Vee Gets

Greek:
Πώς είσαι (**Pós eísai?**)
🦻 Pos ee-say

31
TELL SOMEONE THIS JOKE:

Comic Sans and Arial walk
into a bar.
'Oi,' the bartender says, 'We don't
want your type in here!'

32

UNSCRAMBLE THIS ANAGRAM!

D
O

GONE SURE

(What we should all strive to be)

AROUND THE WORLD

The major religions throughout the world are:

Religion	Estimated no. of worshippers	Date established
Buddhism	520 million	c. 6000–4000 BCE
Christianity	2.4 billion	1st century CE
Hinduism	1.1 billion	c. 1500 BCE with roots as far back as 15000 BCE
Islam	1.8 billion	7th century CE
Judaism	15 million	c. 1800 BCE
Sikhism	25 million	1469

WHAT DID YOU SAY?

Translate the below word using the Morse Code dictionary:

```
A ●▬              U ●●▬
B ▬●●●            V ●●●▬
C ▬●▬●            W ●▬▬
D ▬●●             X ▬●●▬
E ●               Y ▬●▬▬
F ●●▬●            Z ▬▬●●
G ▬▬●
H ●●●●
I ●●
J ●▬▬▬
K ▬●▬             1 ●▬▬▬▬
L ●▬●●            2 ●●▬▬▬
M ▬▬              3 ●●●▬▬
N ▬●              4 ●●●●▬
O ▬▬▬             5 ●●●●●
P ●▬▬●            6 ▬●●●●
Q ▬▬●▬            7 ▬▬●●●
R ●▬●             8 ▬▬▬●●
S ●●●             9 ▬▬▬▬●
T ▬               0 ▬▬▬▬▬
```

▬●▬● ●▬● ●▬ ▬●▬● ▬●▬ ●● ▬● ▬▬●

QUIZ CORNER: MUSIC

A) Which famous pop and rock artist was born Reg Dwight?

B) Who sang 'The Times They Are A-Changin'?

C) Who was given the nickname 'Father of Rock and Roll'?

D) What are the first names of the five original members of One Direction?

E) Who is considered to be the 'Queen of K-pop'?

F) Who out of these artists has not sung a James Bond theme song? Tina Turner, Sam Smith, Whitney Houston or Duran Duran?

G) Who sang 'Je ne regrette rien'?

H) Who set up the record label #MERKY Records?

I) Which group was Chrissie Hynde the lead singer of?

J) Which singer 'Just Called to Say I Love You' in 1984?

LEARN THE US PRESIDENTS

1. George Washington (1789–1797)
2. John Adams (1797–1801)
3. Thomas Jefferson (1801–1809)
4. James Madison (1809–1817)
5. James Monroe (1817–1825)
6. John Quincy Adams (1825–1829)
7. Andrew Jackson (1829–1837)
8. Martin Van Buren (1837–1841)
9. William Henry Harrison (1841)
10. John Tyler (1841–1845)
11. James K. Polk (1845–1849)
12. Zachary Taylor (1849–1850)
13. Millard Fillmore (1850–1853)
14. Franklin Pierce (1853–1857)
15. James Buchanan (1857–1861)
16. Abraham Lincoln (1861–1865)
17. Andrew Johnson (1865–1869)
18. Ulysses S. Grant (1869–1877)
19. Rutherford B. Hayes (1877–1881)
20. James A. Garfield (1881)
21. Chester A. Arthur (1881–1885)
22. Grover Cleveland (1885–1889)
23. Benjamin Harrison (1889–1893)

24. Grover Cleveland (1893–1897)
25. William McKinley (1897–1901)
26. Theodore Roosevelt (1901–1909)
27. William Howard Taft (1909–1913)
28. Woodrow Wilson (1913–1921)
29. Warren G. Harding (1921–1923)
30. Calvin Coolidge (1923–1929)
31. Herbert Hoover (1929–1933)
32. Franklin D. Roosevelt (1933–1945)
33. Harry S. Truman (1945–1953)
34. Dwight D. Eisenhower (1953–1961)
35. John F. Kennedy (1961–1963)
36. Lyndon B. Johnson (1963–1969)
37. Richard Nixon (1969–1974)
38. Gerald Ford (1974–1977)
39. Jimmy Carter (1977–1981)
40. Ronald Reagan (1981–1989)
41. George H. W. Bush (1989–1993)
42. Bill Clinton (1993–2001)
43. George W. Bush (2001–2009)
44. Barack Obama (2009–2017)
45. Donald Trump

WORD SPLURGE!

Make as many different words as you can from the following letters:

YOU ARE FABULOUS

POETRY CORNER

Learn, write out or send on the below:

For Whom The Bell Tolls
John Donne

No man is an island,
Entire of itself.
Each is a piece of the continent,
A part of the main.
If a clod be washed away by the sea,
Europe is the less.
As well as if a promontory were.
As well as if a manor of thine own
Or of thine friend's were.
Each man's death diminishes me,
For I am involved in mankind.
Therefore, send not to know
For whom the bell tolls,
It tolls for thee.

Fun fact: John Donne wrote these words in 1924 in his *Devotions Upon Emergent Occasions*, when he was Dean of St Paul's and after experiencing a very serious case of spotted fever. Rather than write it as a poem, he actually called it Meditation XVII. Another fun fact: Ernest Hemingway then borrowed the title of one of his books in 1940.

39

POP THIS BOOK DOWN AND...

... Do some light exercises to get your energy levels up:

- Jog on the spot for thirty seconds
- Five Star Jumps
- Make ten snow angels on the floor
- Twenty little jumps on the spot
- Hop on one leg ten times
- Hop on the other leg ten times
- Repeat!

40
IN A NUTSHELL: PREHISTORIC TIMES

2.8 million years ago: Our ancestors, the *Homo,* evolve

2.5 million years ago: They start making tools

400,000 years ago: They discover fire

200,000 years ago: Homo sapiens are now existing in Africa

c. 170,000 years ago: We start wearing clothes

75,000 years ago: The Toba volcano in Indonesia erupts in
    what is known as a super-eruption, leaving a 15cm layer
    of ash over the whole of South Asia

80,000 – 50,000 years ago: We migrate out of Africa,
    gradually reaching southern India, the Malay islands,
    Australia, Japan, China, Siberia, Alaska and the north
    west of North America

80,000 – 50,000 years ago: We start using language

40,000 years ago: Neanderthals go extinct

26,500 years ago: the last glaciers in Western Europe
    retreat – we migrate there and can enter North America
    from Eastern Siberia.

13–15,000 years ago: A climate cycle known as 'The African
    humid period' means that the Sahara is wet and fertile

9,000 years ago: Agriculture has by now begun: figs are
    being cultivated in the Jordan Valley near Jericho

8000–7000 BCE: Wheat and barley is cultivated in
    Mesopotamia (part of modern Iraq)

8000 BCE: We build using bricks for the first time

6000 BCE: We start making boats

3500 BCE: We make glass

3500-3000 BCE: In Mesopotamia, we develop the first
written language: Cuneiform

3000 BCE: The building of Stonehenge in England begins

UNSCRAMBLE THIS ANAGRAM!

GRUNT RUIN

(Caring for someone
or something)

RIDDLE ME THIS:

Where does age always come before beauty?

QUIZ CORNER: FLAGS

A) How many stars are on China's flag?

B) What colours are on Greece's flag?

C) What type of leaf is on the Canada flag?

D) Which country's flag features a dragon?

E) What are the colours of the Irish flag and what is the correct order that they appear in from left to right?

F) How many colours are featured on the South African flag?

G) Which of the following countries do NOT have blue in their flag: Argentina, Cuba, Iran or Brazil?

H) Which of the following countries do NOT have at least one star on their flag: Singapore, Nigeria, Vietnam or Panama?

I) Which of the following countries do NOT have a cross on their flag: Switzerland, Luxembourg, Norway or Sweden?

J) Which of the following countries has a crescent moon on its flag: Yemen, Turkey, Zimbabwe or Russia?

44
AROUND THE WORLD

Different nationalities practice different customs, habits and traditions. How many of the below had you heard of or seen before?

Nicaragua: Nicaraguans don't point with their finger or thumb; instead they use puckered lips to gesture in the direction they're talking about.

Greece: Spitting is traditionally considered to be good luck in Greece and would happen often at weddings and baptisms. Today the Greeks don't do it literally, but instead say 'ftou ftou'.

Denmark: Cemeteries act like parks in Denmark and are often well-tended areas where people socialise.

Japan: Making slurping sounds whilst you eat is considered a grateful sign that you're enjoying your food.

Egypt: It's rude to ask for salt when you're eating in Egypt as it's interpreted that you don't like your meal.

Philippines: In Filipino culture it's common for villagers to lift and move whole houses to a completely new place (often to get the house out of the way of oncoming floods or other natural phenomenon). It's a tradition closely linked with *bayanihan* – or community – spirit.

WOULD YOU RATHER . . .

Would you rather kiss a frog or stroke a tarantula?

Would you rather have the top half of a human and the bottom half of a cat, or the other way around?

Would you rather live in a lighthouse on an island or a treehouse in a rainforest?

Would you rather have the hearing of a bat or the eyesight of a falcon?

Would you rather give the stranger on the bus next to you £1 million or receive £50,000 yourself?

Would you rather lose one finger on one hand, or all your toes on one foot?

Would you rather go back in time or to the future?

Would you rather have two noses or two mouths?

Would you rather live in an old airport or an old train station?

Would you rather live in Ancient Egypt or Victorian Britain?

46

POPTASTIC

The Eurovision song contest has been running since 1965. In some countries it's now considered something of a joke, but it's still a mainstay of the calendar year for many others and is a great way of bringing countries of the world together. Here are some of our favourite winners – give them a watch and see whether you too would have given them douze points!

Year	Country	Act	Song	Fun fact
1968	Spain	Massiel	La, la, la	Massiel's cheery display will not only get stuck in your head for days on end, she also beat Cliff Richard's 'Congratulations' to get the top gong. ▶

1974	Sweden	Abba	Waterloo	In 2005, 'Waterloo' was chosen as the best Eurovision entry in the contest's then 50-year history, and it's also one of the best-selling singles of all time.
1976	UK	Brotherhood of Man	Save Your Kisses for Me	Whoever came up with that dance routine was inspired, and just wait for the moment when Martin Lee winks at the camera ...
1988	Switzerland	Celine Dion	Ne Partez Pas Sans Moi	It's unusual now for established artists to take part in the contest, but Celine Dion did back in the eighties at the start of her career, and her entry narrowly scooped the top prize by just one point.

Year	Country	Artist	Song	Notes
1998	Israel	Dana International	Diva	Dana International was the first transgender woman to enter Eurovision with a song that has a catchy chorus which may or may not reference Posh Spice.
2009	Norway	Alexander Rybak	Fairytale	Alexander and his violin scored 387 points – the highest ever total since the contest began.
2013	Denmark	Emmelie de Forest	Only Teardrops	Actually quite a good pop song for recent years, and went to number one in the charts in Denmark.
2014	Austria	Conchita Wurst	Rise Like a Phoenix	Some conservative countries complained about Conchita, which makes it all the more satisfying that she won!

FACT ATTACK

Learn this gem and wow people with your genius

The 'Qwerty' keyboard we have on our laptops and PCs today is the same as the original typewriter, invented in 1868 by Christopher Latham Sholes.

QUIZ CORNER: CHRISTMAS

A) In what century can we see the first written use of 'Xmas'?

B) The French word 'Noël' is often used around Christmas, but what was its original meaning in Latin?

C) On Christmas Day in 1886, which famous landmark did the French gift to America?

D) How many Wise Men/Magi/Kings does the Bible say visited the baby Jesus?

E) Which country donates a Christmas Tree to the British people each year, to stand in Trafalgar Square, London and why?

F) Why is Boxing Day so-called?

G) What is the first line of *A Visit from St Nicholas* by Clement Clarke Moore?

H) How many ghosts feature in Charles Dickens' *A Christmas Carol?*

I) How do you say 'Merry Christmas' in Spanish?

J) In which country do children receive gifts and treats on 5 December (St Nicholas' Eve) each year?

49

TELL SOMEONE THIS JOKE:

I was playing golf with a friend.
'Let's make this interesting,'
he said – so we stopped
playing golf.

AROUND THE WORLD

Learn these capital cities of the world if you haven't heard of them before:

Capital	Place
Kigali	Rwanda
Flying Fish Cove	Christmas Island
Muscat	Oman
Port-au-Prince	Haiti
Tegucigalpa	Honduras
Vilnius	Lithuania
Zagreb	Croatia
Tashkent	Uzbekistan
Rabat	Morocco

51

WHAT DID YOU SAY?

**Translate the below word using the
Morse Code dictionary:**

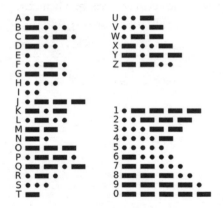

52

POP THIS BOOK DOWN AND . . .

DO

. . . Practise being present. You can do this by putting a piece of chocolate in your mouth and focusing on all the different sensations it causes. How many edges are there, how does your tongue feel, what can you taste, what can you smell, how long is it taking to melt, what else is this piece of chocolate affecting? Or you could go to a window and open it a fraction. Close your eyes and focus on your other senses: what can you feel on your face, what can you smell, what can you hear?

PARROT POWER

Learn, write out or send on this quote:

'No feats of heroism are needed to achieve the greatest and most important changes in the existence of humanity; neither the armament of millions of soldiers, nor the construction of new roads and machines, nor the arrangement of exhibitions, nor the organisation of workmen's unions, nor revolutions, nor barricades, nor explosions, nor the perfection of aerial navigation; but a change in public opinion.'

Fun fact: The Russian writer Leo Tolstoy wrote this in a book called *Patriotism and Christianity*, published in 1896.

IN A NUTSHELL: THE BRONZE AGE

The period from 3300 to 1200 BCE is known as the Bronze Age, so called because it's believed to have been a time when humans were consistently using the metal to improve their lives. Inventions, trade and the rise of states and empires began during these millennia. You will probably know about Ancient Greece but have you heard of Babylonia or Assyria, which were also major players during the Bronze Age? Babylonia existed in present day Iraq and one of its kings, Hammurabi, was responsible for originating one of the world's earliest and most-complete legal codes – almost 4,000 years ago! Assyria, also in present day Iraq, had an empire that extended to Turkey and Egypt (which meant the pharaohs were great rivals to them).

The end of the Bronze Age is marked by the collapse of all of the major civilisations in the region, which historians believe could be down to a string of natural catastrophes.

UNSCRAMBLE THIS ANAGRAM!

OH WE MOLES
(Reading and baking
might be considered activities
in this bracket)

QUIZ CORNER: SHAKESPEARE

A) Who was Shakespeare married to?

B) What were Romeo and Juliet's family names?

C) Which play do Beatrice and Benedick star in?

D) Which play does this quote feature in: 'And this our life exempt from public haunt,/Finds tongues in trees, books in the running brooks, Sermons in stones, and good in everything'?

E) Which Shakespeare play was the Amanda Bynes film *She's the Man* based on?

F) Where was Shakespeare born?

G) What is Shakespeare's shortest play?

H) Which contemporary of Shakespeare first played Hamlet, Othello, King Lear and Richard III?

I) Characters named Balthasar appear in several Shakespeare plays. Which of these does he not exist in? *Romeo and Juliet*, *Othello*, *The Merchant of Venice* or *Much Ado About Nothing*

J) Which pop singer has a namesake in *Richard III*? Will Young, James Blunt or Paul Simon?

LEARN SOME LATIN

Plants and trees are so special that they get two names: the one we refer to them as in everyday life, and the botanical one Carl Linnaeus, a Swedish botanist, insisted they have to distinguish their genus and species. This is useful because there are often many different types of one particular plant (or animal) so it helps us to tell them apart. Here are a few to swot up on.

Common name	Latin name
Orchid	Phalaenopsis
Sunflower	Helianthus
Apple tree	Malus domestica
Daisy	Bellis perennis
Oak tree	Quercus
Snowdrop	Galanthus
Yarrow	Achillea

TELL SOMEONE THIS JOKE:

Doctor: The good news is you
don't have an ear infection.
Patient: I'd like a second opinion.
Doctor: Well, since you asked,
you *do* have bad breath.

SAY HELLO TO YOUR HUMAN RIGHTS

In 1948 – in the wake of the horrors of WWII – the newly formed United Nations formed the Universal Declaration of Human Rights with the aim of establishing a code that all countries in the world would adhere to. Various countries have enshrined the below human rights into their own laws, and the fight goes on to get the rest to abide by them.

Article 1: All humans are free and equal.

Article 2: All humans, regardless of any sort of distinction (including but not limited to race, colour, sex, wealth and political affiliation) are entitled to these rights.

Article 3: Everyone has the right to life, liberty and safety.

Article 4: No one shall be a slave.

Article 5: No one shall be tortured or subjected to degrading treatment or punishment.

Article 6: Everyone is recognised as a person before the law.

Article 7: Everyone is equal before the law and should be protected by the law.

Article 8: If one of these rights is denied to a person or violated, then that person has the right to challenge that action via the law.

Article 9: No one shall be arrested, exiled or put into detention without a cause.

Article 10: Everyone is entitled to a fair trial.

Article 11: Everyone is to be considered innocent until proven guilty. No one shall be prosecuted for something they did which was not a crime at the point of action.

Article 12: Everyone has the right to privacy, family life, home and correspondence without fear of arbitrary interference from the authorities.

Article 13: Everyone is free to move within their own country, to leave their own country and to return.

Article 14: Everyone has right to seek asylum from prosecution in other countries.

Article 15: Everyone has the right to a nationality. No one shall have that nationality taken away without good reason, or be refused a chance to change their nationality.

Article 16: Consenting adults have the right to marry and to start a family no matter their race, nationality or religion. Marriage should not be forced on any person who does not consent, and both persons are entitled to equal rights during the marriage and if it should end.

Article 17: Everyone has the right to own property and they shall not be arbitrarily deprived of it.

Article 18: Everyone has the right to religion, and to choose, change and practise their religion in public and in private.

Article 19: Everyone has the right to free thought and expression and to impart this to others.

Article 20: Everyone has the right to gather and form groups peacefully.

Article 21: Each country's government's authority is based on the will of the people and therefore each government will be voted in through fair elections. All citizens shall be allowed to vote and to take part in the government of their country, either directly or through elected representatives.

Article 22: Everyone has the right to social security and to pursue economic, social and cultural fulfilment.

Article 23: Everyone has the right to work, to receive equal pay for equal work and to form and join trade unions to protect workers' interests.

Article 24: Everyone has the right to rest and leisure.

Article 25: Everyone has the right to an adequate standard of living for themselves and their family and the right to security if circumstances beyond their control results in loss of livelihood. Motherhood and childhood, no matter the circumstances, are entitled to special care and assistance.

Article 26: Everyone has the right to free elementary education, which shall be compulsory. Higher education shall be accessible to all on the basis of merit. Education shall not promote intolerance of any nation or group of people, but instead encourage understanding and friendship between all countries, races and religious groups.

Article 27: Everyone has the right to participate in cultural life and to benefit morally and materially from any scientific, literary or artistic production they have originated.

Article 28: Everyone has the right to live in a society where the above rights are recognised.

Article 29: Everyone has the right to live as their personality dictates, so long as it respects the rights, freedoms and protections of all others within society.

Article 30: None of the above may be interpreted in a way that would allow any government, group or person to obstruct any of the rights and freedoms that are listed here.

RIDDLE ME THIS:

D
O

What can you break without
ever touching it?

POETRY CORNER

Learn, write out or send on the below:

To Mrs Reynold's Cat
John Keats

Cat! who has pass'd thy grand climacteric
How many mice and rats hast in thy days
Destroy'd? – how many tit bits stolen? Gaze
With those bright languid segments green and prick
Those velvet ears – but pr'ythee do not stick
Thy latent talons in me – and upraise
Thy gentle mew – and tell me all thy frays
Of fish and mice, and rats and tender chick.
Nay, look not down, nor lick thy dainty wrists –
For all the wheezy asthma – and for all
Thy tail's tip is nicked off – and though the fists
Of many a maid have given thee many a maul,
Still is that fur as soft as when the lists
In youth thou enter'dst on glass-bottled wall.

Fun fact: Keats wrote this poem in 1818. Mrs Reynolds was the wife of his good friend John Hamilton Reynolds, and there's something lovely about imagining him writing this whilst the cat sits in front of him or on his lap, digging his claws in!

QUIZ CORNER: DISNEY

A) What animal is Timon from *The Lion King*?

B) What was the first feature length film to be released by Disney?

C) Which film featured the songs 'Reflection' and 'I'll Make a Man Out of You'?

D) Who lives on the Polynesian island of Motunui?

E) Which fairytale features 'Bibbidi-Bobbidi-Boo'?

F) What's been Disney's highest-grossing film to date? *Avengers: Endgame*, *Frozen* or *Star Wars: The Last Jedi*?

G) In *Aladdin*, how long was the Genie stuck in the lamp for?

H) What is the name of Cinderella's stepmother's nasty cat?

I) Who is the only Disney main character to not talk once in the film they are in?

J) Who is Buzz Lightyear's nemesis?

UNSCRAMBLE THIS ANAGRAM!

NOBLE EVENT

(Very, very kind)

64
FIRST AMONG FOLKS

LEARN

The first person to go into space was Yuri Alekseyevich Gagarin, on 12 April 1961. He was only twenty-seven years old and he became the first person to orbit the planet, which took a total of eighty-nine minutes.

WORD SPLURGE

Make as many different words as you can from the following letters:

BELIEVE IN YOURSELF

L
E
A
R
N

AROUND THE WORLD

**Learn these currencies if you haven't
heard of them before ...**

Country	Currency	Symbol
Brazil	Brazilian real	R$
Cuba	Cuban peso	$
Egypt	Egyptian pound	£ or ج.م
Hungary	Hungarian forint	Ft
Macau	Macanese pataca	P
Papua New Guinea	Papua New Guinean kina	K
Somalia	Somali shilling	Sh
Tonga	Tonga pa'anga	T$
Turkmenistan	Turkmenistan manat	m
Zambia	Zambian kwacha	ZK

67

PARROT POWER

Learn, write out or send on this quote:

'Another world is not only possible, she is on her way. On a quiet day, I can hear her breathing.'

Fun fact: Arundhati Roy, perhaps best known for her debut novel *The God of Small Things* which won the Booker Prize in 1997, wrote the above quote in *An Ordinary Person's Guide to Empire,* published in 2005.

CAN YOU COME UP WITH A...

D
O

... Spoonerism? A spoonerism is a purposeful funny verbal error, where certain letters of one word are swapped with another to change the meaning. For example 'nosy little cook' instead of 'cosy little nook'.

69

FOOD FOR THOUGHT!

Do you know which country each of the following dishes are associated with?

A) Moules Frites

B) Pastel de Choclo

C) Khachapuri

D) Goulash

E) Haggis

F) Doner Kebab

G) Pho

H) Cou Cou

QUIZ CORNER: OSCAR WINNERS

A) Which of these films did not win a Best Picture Oscar? *Spotlight, The King's Speech, Avatar* or *Crash*?

B) What record did *Parasite* break when it won Best Picture at the Oscars in 2020?

C) What film did Juliette Binoche win Best Supporting Actress for?

D) What did Adrien Brody controversially do when he won his Best Actor Oscar for *The Pianist* back in 2002?

E) Which song from *The Little Mermaid* won the Oscar for Original Song in 1989?

F) Steve McQueen was the first black director to win Best Picture for which film?

G) Three films have won the 'big five' Oscars – Best Picture, Director, Actor, Actress and Screenplay. Can you name one of them?

H) In 2009, Kathryn Bigelow became the first woman to win Best Director – what was the film?

WHAT A GEM

You may think that 'birthstones' are a cynical invention by jewellers to encourage consumerism – and you'd be half right! The below standardised list was decided in 1912 by the Jewelers of America association. BUT there's evidence that the tradition originated in Biblical times, and from various places around the world. Which gemstone are you?

Month	Birthstone
January	Garnet
February	Amethyst
March	Aquamarine, bloodstone
April	Diamond
May	Emerald
June	Pearl, moonstone
July	Ruby, carnelian
August	Peridot, sardonyx
September	Sapphire, lapis lazuli
October	Opal
November	Topaz, Citrine
December	Tanzanite, turquoise

72

POP THIS BOOK DOWN AND...

... Write and send a letter to someone you haven't seen lately – It could be a thank you letter, a thinking of you letter or just a letter saying hello!

UNSCRAMBLE THIS ANAGRAM!

MODEL BEN

(To buoy someone up)

AGE BEFORE BEAUTY!

Many of the animals that populate the earth go back millions of years; some were even around at the time of the dinosaurs, who ruled the roost for 160 million years until they were wiped out roughly 65.5 million years ago. How many of the below examples did you know already?

The crocodiles and their close ancestors have been around for about 85 million years, and they belonged to an even bigger group called 'crocodylomorpha' which originated over 205 million years ago!

The platypus is a very special mammal whose roots go back a great deal further than most of its fellows. Fossils of its relative, the obdurodon, have been found in rocks that are between 5 and 25 million years old.

Sharks began evolving 450 million years ago, before even trees existed! But it wasn't until 380 million years ago that the Cladoselache evolved which is the first group we would recognise as a shark (even though technically speaking scientists aren't sure it's part of the 'shark' family).

The horseshoe crab takes the prize – it's been around for about 450 million years, probably because it has such an effective immune system.

WORD SPLURGE

Make as many different words as you can from the following letters:

THE TIME IS NOW

76

FIRST AMONG FOLKS

LEARN

You decide: usually the first people credited with flying are the Wright Brothers (Wilbur and Orville) but they might have been beaten to it by Gustave Whitehead, who invented a flying car in 1901 and is believed to have flown it the same year to a height of fifty feet.

77
RIDDLE ME THIS:

I go into the hairdressers'
every day but my hair never
gets any shorter. Why?

QUIZ CORNER: GEOGRAPHY

D
O

A) What's the longest river in the world?

B) What continent are the Andes in?

C) What type of rock is limestone?

D) What is the imaginary line that runs between the North and South Pole called?

E) What is the smallest country in the world?

F) What is the name given to the outermost shell of Earth (and other planets), which includes the crust and upper mantle?

G) Which country in Europe shares its borders with nine other countries?

H) Which city is known as Baile Atha Cliath in Gaelic?

I) What is the tallest natural waterfall in the world?

J) Which of these countries is *not* in the southern hemisphere: Mauritius, Thailand, Uruguay or Angola?

79

PARROT POWER

Learn, write out or send on this quote:

'Carry out a random act of kindness, with no expectation of reward, safe in the knowledge that one day someone might do the same for you.'

Diana, Princess of Wales

TELL SOMEONE THIS JOKE:

Two giraffes want to
cross the road.
'Shall we do it now?' one says.
'Not a chance,' the other says.
'Look what happened to
that zebra.'

POP THIS BOOK DOWN AND...

... Make (then listen to) this positive playlist:

Johnny Nash – 'I Can See Clearly Now'

Natalie Cole – 'This Will Be (An Everlasting Love)'

Pharrell Williams – 'Happy'

Bobby McFerrin – 'Don't Worry Be Happy'

Bob Marley – 'Three Little Birds'

Frank Wilson – 'Do I Love You'

Leo Sayer – 'You Make Me Feel Like Dancing'

Katrina and the Waves – 'Walking on Sunshine'

Jimmy Durante – 'Make Someone Happy'

Rusted Root – 'Send Me On My Way'

IN A NUTSHELL: THE IRON AGE

The Iron Age as a concept is flawed, because different regions around the world were advancing at different rates during the years it concerns. But traditionally speaking, it covers the Ancient Near East (roughly the modern Middle East) and Europe during the years 1200 BCE to roughly 550 BCE when historic records began. It is so-called because it was a time when iron and steel were used to make tools and weapons that were better than their bronze predecessors. It was during the Iron Age that Classical Greece (think Athens, Sparta, philosophers and democracy) flourished, as well as the expansive Persian Empire. Further west, things were more tribal. Celts across Britain, Ireland, France, Spain and elsewhere lived in hill forts, spreading similar languages and Druid religious beliefs.

WHAT DID YOU SAY?

Translate the below word using the Morse Code dictionary:

84

CAN YOU COME UP WITH A...

...Portmanteau? A portmanteau is where two words have been blended together to create a new word. For example 'brunch' is a portmanteau of breakfast and lunch.

POETRY CORNER

Learn, write out or send on the below:

Love Shook My Heart
Sappho

Love shook my heart,
Like the wind on the mountain
Troubling the oak trees.

Fun Fact: Sappho was considered to be one of the greatest poets in ancient Greece – she lived over 2,500 years ago! Much of her poetry is lost, but various fragments survive. Her poems were designed to be sung to a tune played by a lyre.

QUIZ CORNER: DINOSAURS

A) What was a 'sauropod'?

B) Which came first: Stegosaurus or Tyrannosaurus?

C) How do scientists estimate a dinosaur's leg-length by looking at a footprint?

D) What purpose did feathers serve dinosaurs?

E) What type of teeth did the Tyrannosaurus have?

F) How long did dinosaurs walk the earth for?

G) What was a 'pterodactyl'?

H) What did a velociraptor eat?

I) Which dinosaur is considered to be the tallest (and probably the tallest animal to have ever walked the earth)?

J) What does the word 'dinosaur' mean?

87

POP THIS BOOK DOWN AND . . .

. . . Go tidy your pants drawer – first, take all your pants out. Second, throw away the grubby, holey specimens. Third, roll up each pair width-ways. Then neatly wedge each one back into your drawer, and enjoy until it's messy once more.

88

SWOT UP ON YOUR SHAKESPEARE

Not everyone is a fan of Shakespeare so instead of discussing his plays, let's focus on what we can all agree he was brilliant at: insults. Keep these in your arsenal for when the occasion rises:

'His wit's as thick as a Tewkesbury mustard.'
Henry IV Part 2 (Act 2, Scene 4)

'More of your conversation would infect my brain.'
Coriolanus (Act 2, Scene 1)

'The rankest compound of villainous smell that ever offended nostril.'
The Merry Wives of Windsor (Act 3, Scene 5)

'Thou art as fat as butter.'
Henry IV Part 1 (Act 2, Scene 4)

'Would you wert clean enough to spit upon.'
Timon of Athens (Act 4, Scene 3)

'The tartness of his face sours ripe grapes.'
Coriolanus (Act 5, Scene 4)

POETRY CORNER

Learn, write out or send on the below:

An Hymn to the Morning
Phillis Wheatley

Attend my lays, ye ever honour'd nine,
Assist my labours, and my strains refine;
In smoothest numbers pour the notes along,
For bright Aurora now demands my song.
Aurora hail, and all the thousand dies,
Which deck thy progress through the vaulted skies:
The morn awakes, and wide extends her rays,
On ev'ry leaf the gentle zephyr plays;
Harmonious lays the feather'd race resume,
Dart the bright eye, and shake the painted plume.
Ye shady groves, your verdant gloom display
To shield your poet from the burning day:
Calliope awake the sacred lyre,
While thy fair sisters fan the pleasing fire:
The bow'rs, the gales, the variegated skies
In all their pleasures in my bosom rise.
See in the east th' illustrious king of day!
His rising radiance drives the shades away –

But Oh! I feel his fervid beams too strong,
And scarce begun, concludes th' abortive song.

Fun fact: Phillis Wheatley was the first African-American woman to publish a book of poetry (in 1773). Born in West Africa, she was sold into slavery as a child. Her 'owners', a family in Boston called the Wheatleys, taught her to read and write and encouraged her poetry. Whilst she was emancipated shortly after her poetry published, at the time of writing she was still a slave.

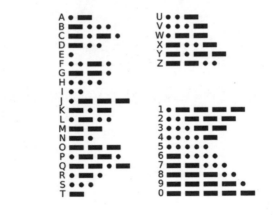

WHAT DID YOU SAY?

Translate the below word using the Morse Code dictionary:

UNSCRAMBLE THIS ANAGRAM!

BRAVO NEST

(Take a look out of the window)

FIRST AMONG FOLKS

Over ninety years after the Nobel Prize for literature was established, the first black woman was awarded it in 1993. She was Toni Morrison for her much-acclaimed book *Beloved*.

CAN YOU COME UP WITH A . . .

... Paraprosdokian? A paraprosdokian is where the second half of a sentence is surprising given what's just been said. For example 'He was always so brilliant at being a loser'.

FACT ATTACK

Learn this gem and wow people with your genius

The oldest human permanent settlement that we know of is between 23 and 25 thousand years old. Archaeologists found the huts made from rocks alongside mammoth bones (suggesting these people hunted mammoths) in Moravia in the Czech Republic.

QUIZ CORNER: FRIENDS SPECIAL!

A) Whose alias is Regina Phalange?

B) What's Joey's penguin called?

C) Who was Barry?

D) Who danced with their head inside a turkey?

E) What was Chandler's job in the first few seasons?

F) What animal does Ross plan to buy with Julie?

G) Who sang the Friends theme song?

H) What are Ross and Monica's parents called?

I) What scares the 'bejesus' out of Chandler?

J) Who are Theodore and Dilsy?

POP THIS BOOK DOWN AND...

...Write a short story using one of the starting lines below:

Out at sea, there was only one thing you could eat for breakfast.

Whilst the storm raged on outside, inside the fire crackled in its grate.

The cloud was a comfortable place to lounge on whilst you watched the countries below drift by.

97

FIRST AMONG FOLKS

The first person to have been born after conception by IVF (in vitro fertilisation) was Louise Joy Brown at Oldham General Hospital in Manchester, England in 1978.

AROUND THE WORLD

Whilst Asia is the continent with the most amount of people in the world, Africa is the continent with the most amount of countries. Can you learn them all?

No.	Country	Population in millions	Area
1	Nigeria	200	Western Africa
2	Ethiopia	115	Eastern Africa
3	Egypt	102	Northern Africa
4	DR Congo	90	Middle Africa
5	Tanzania	60	Eastern Africa
6	South Africa	59	Southern Africa
7	Kenya	54	Eastern Africa
8	Uganda	46	Eastern Africa
9	Algeria	44	Northern Africa
10	Sudan	44	Northern Africa
11	Morocco	37	Northern Africa
12	Angola	33	Middle Africa

13	Mozambique	33	Eastern Africa
14	Ghana	31	Western Africa
15	Madagascar	28	Eastern Africa
16	Cameroon	27	Middle Africa
17	Côte d'Ivoire	26	Western Africa
18	Niger	24	Western Africa
19	Burkina Faso	21	Western Africa
20	Mali	20	Western Africa
21	Malawi	19	Eastern Africa
22	Zambia	18	Eastern Africa
23	Senegal	17	Western Africa
24	Chad	16	Middle Africa
25	Somalia	16	Eastern Africa
26	Zimbabwe	15	Eastern Africa
27	Guinea	13	Western Africa
28	Rwanda	13	Eastern Africa
29	Benin	12	Western Africa
30	Burundi	12	Eastern Africa
31	Tunisia	12	Northern Africa
32	South Sudan	11	Eastern Africa
33	Togo	8	Western Africa
34	Sierra Leone	8	Western Africa
35	Libya	7	Northern Africa
36	Congo	6	Middle Africa

▶

37	Liberia	5	Western Africa
38	Central African Republic	5	Middle Africa
39	Mauritania	5	Western Africa
40	Eritrea	4	Eastern Africa
41	Namibia	3	Southern Africa
42	Gambia	2	Western Africa
43	Botswana	2	Southern Africa
44	Gabon	2	Middle Africa
45	Lesotho	2	Southern Africa
46	Guinea-Bissau	2	Western Africa
47	Equatorial Guinea	1	Middle Africa
48	Mauritius	1	Eastern Africa
49	Eswatini	1	Southern Africa
50	Djibouti	1	Eastern Africa
51	Comoros	0.9	Eastern Africa
52	Cabo Verde	0.5	Western Africa
53	Sao Tome & Principe	0.2	Middle Africa
54	Seychelles	0.1	Eastern Africa

99
FACT ATTACK

L E A R N

Learn this gem and wow people with your genius

Experts say the average trained dog can understand around 165 words, and very intelligent dogs can even learn up to 200 (that's roughly the same as a two-year-old!).

100

AROUND THE WORLD

How to say 'I love you' in other languages

Scottish Gaelic: tha gaol agam ort
🕉 Ha g-eul ah-kum orsht

Burmese: မင်္ဂလာကိုခွျစ်တယ် (mainnkohkyittaal)
🕉 meh-ko-chet-ay

Swahili: nakupenda
🕉 na-koo-pennn-da

Spanish: Te quiero
🕉 Tay Key-ro

French: Je t'aime
🕉 Jer tem

Irish: tá mé i ngrá leat
🕉 Taw may ih ngra lee-at

UNSCRAMBLE THIS ANAGRAM!

D
O

I UNCLE VIS

(You're welcome at

our party any time)

ANSWERS

1)

A. Machu Picchu in Peru dates from the 1400s whilst the Taj Mahal was built in the 1600s.

B. Construction of the Eiffel Tower began in 1887; the Empire State began in 1930.

C. Donald Trump was born in 1946 and Vladimir Putin was born in 1952.

D. Justin Bieber was born on 1 March 1994 and Harry Styles was born on 1 February 1994 – only a month apart!

E. Construction began on the Sydney Opera House in 1959 (although wasn't completed until 1973!) and the Lotus Temple began in 1986.

F. Angkor Wat was built in the 12th century whilst St Basil's Cathedral was built in the 16th century.

G. Construction started on Buckingham Palace in 1703 whilst building of Versailles began in 1631.

H. The Leaning Tower of Pisa began its life in 1173; construction of the Forbidden City was begun in the 1400s.

I. J. K. Rowling was born in 1965 whilst Neil Gaiman was born in 1960.

J. Beyoncé was born in 1981 whilst David Beckham was born in 1975.

2) Champion

4)

A. Venus – at 450°C!

B. Andromeda Galaxy

C. In 2006, scientists established clearer rules about what categorised a 'planet'. Because of these new rules, Pluto was demoted from planet to dwarf planet because it's not big enough to exert orbital dominance on other objects in its neighbourhood

D. 4.6 billion years

E. 13.8 billion years ago. Scientists have estimated this date based on their measurements of the expansion rate of the universe.

F. The Soviet Union's Sputnik in 1957, triggering the Space Race

G. Because Jupiter doesn't have a solid surface!

H. Because there's no wind in space.

I. Saturn

J. It's a telescope, named after the astronomer Edwin Hubble, that was launched into space by Nasa in 1990 and is still providing us with information today.

6) A clock

13) Playful

14)
A. 91
B. 33
C. 8 packs
D. 10.5 miles
E. 6/8
F. Book on the floor = 10cm. Table = 50cm
G. 60°
H. 0

16) Effervescent

18) A bank

20)
A. Mongol Empire
B. First half of the 14th century
C. The Giza Pyramids are believed to have been built between 2589 and 2504, making them over 4,500 years old
D. The Confederates (made up of eleven southern states who left the Union in 1860 and 1861) and the Unionists (the north).
E. Bastille Day is celebrated in France on 14 July each year. It commemorates the storming of the Bastille, a fortress and prison in Paris, which took place on 14 July 1789 and is considered a turning point in the French Revolution.
F. Winchester
G. Cheng I Sao was a 19th century pirate. She had hundreds of ships and 50,000 men under her command, and she wrote a strict code of conduct to keep her pirate followers in line.
H. Peru
I. 1994
J. 1989

22)
A. Poland
B. Iceland

C. Japan
D. Greenland
E. Madagascar
F. Spain

26) Harmonious

29)
A. Hilary Mantel – for *Wolf Hall* in 2009 and *Bring Up the Bodies* in 2012
B. Winston Smith
C. His Dark Materials by Philip Pullman
D. US Declaration of Independence
E. *I Capture the Castle*
F. Victor Hugo's *Les Miserables*
G. Roald Dahl
H. 1997
I. The Danish author Hans Christian Andersen is best known for writing fairy tales – he wrote 3,381!
J. The Bible

32) Generous

34) Cracking

35)
A. Elton John
B. Bob Dylan
C. Chuck Berry
D. Harry, Louis, Liam, Niall, Zayn
E. Kwon Bo-ah
F. Whitney Houston
G. Edith Piaf
H. Stormzy
I. The Pretenders
J. Stevie Wonder

41) Nurturing

42) The dictionary

43)
A. Five – one big, four small
B. Blue and white
C. Maple leaf
D. Wales
E. Green, white, orange
F. Six – red, white, green, yellow, black and blue
G. Iran
H. Nigeria
I. Luxembourg
J. Turkey

48)
A. 16th Century
B. Birth
C. The Statue of Liberty
D. Trick question! It doesn't mention a number
E. Norway. The city of Oslo gifts it each year in gratitude for British support to Norway in WWII.
F. Boxing Day became known as such because the day after Christmas the money left in church alms-boxes for the poor was collected.
G. 'Twas the night before Christmas, when all through the house'
H. Four
I. Feliz Navidad
J. The Netherlands

51) Ergonomic

55) Wholesome

56)
A. Anne Hathaway
B. Montague and Capulet respectively
C. *Much Ado About Nothing*
D. *As You Like It*
E. *Twelfth Night*
F. Stratford-upon-Avon, England
G. *The Comedy of Errors*
H. Richard Burbage

I) Othello
J) James Blunt – he's a supporter of the Earl of Richmond, the future Henry VII

60) A promise

62)
A. Meerkat
B. *Snow White and the Seven Dwarfs*
C. *Mulan*
D. Moana
E. *Cinderella*
F. *Avengers: Endgame*
G. 10,000 years
H. Lucifer
I. Dumbo
J. Zurg

63) Benevolent

69)
A. Belgium is famous for a steaming bowl of mussels with chips on the side.
B. Pastel de Choclo is associated with Chile. It's a pie that includes ground beef, onions, olives and raisins and the crust on top is made from sweetcorn kernels.
C. Khachapuri is famous within Georgia. It's a type of bread filled with cheese and topped with a cracked soft-boiled egg and butter.
D. Hungary is famous for this meat stew made with tomatoes, paprika, noodles and potatoes.
E. Haggis is made from spiced sheep's heart, liver and lungs fried with onions.
F. Turkey is famous for bread filled with sliced crisp beef and salad.
G. A well-seasoned broth with rice noodles is a popular dish within Vietnam.
H. This is a thick cornmeal and okra porridge eaten in Barbados, often topped with a flying fish curry.

70)

A. *Avatar*

B. It was the first film not in English to receive the award.

C. *The English Patient*

D. Adrien grabbed Halle Berry – who was presenting him with the award – and kissed her on the lips!

E. 'Under the Sea'

F. *12 Years a Slave*

G. *It Happened One Night, One Flew Over the Cuckoo's Nest* and *The Silence of the Lambs*

H. *The Hurt Locker*

73) Embolden

77) I work there

78)

A. The Nile

B. South America

C. Sedimentary

D. Prime Meridian

E. Vatican City

F. Lithosphere

G. Germany

H. Dublin

I) Angel Falls in Venezuela

J) Thailand

83) Blessings

86)

A. A four-legged, long-necked herbivore dinosaur

B. Stegosaurus – it was extinct for 66 million years before the Tyrannosaurs arrived!

C. They multiply the length of the footprint by four.

D. Scientists think it could have been either to attract a mate or to keep them warm.

E. They were pointed, slightly curved and serrated.

F. A whopping 165 million years!

G. A winged reptile that could fly and which lived at the same time as some of the dinosaurs – but it was not in fact a dinosaur itself.

H. Velociraptors were carnivores – so they probably would have eaten small dinosaurs and mammals, reptiles, amphibians, insects and other small animals they could catch.

I) Sauroposeidon, which scientists believe could have reached about 18.5 metres in height.

J) Terrible lizard

90) Distinguished

91) Observant

95)
A. Phoebe
B. Hugsy
C. The dentist Rachel decided not to marry at the beginning of series one
D. Monica
E. IT procurements manager
F. A cat
G. The Remembrandts
H. Jack and Judy
I. Michael Flatley, Lord of the Dance
J. Mike's parents

101) Inclusive